Table of Contents

Chapter 1: Mindful Melodies: A Symphony for Inner Harmony

Introduction

In the fast-paced, modern world, where the demands of life can often feel overwhelming, cultivating a calm mind has become a valuable skill. Understanding the importance of a calm mind and embracing techniques to achieve it can significantly enhance both mental and physical well-being. This introduction sets the stage for exploring the transformative benefits of calming the mind.

Understanding the Importance of a Calm Mind

In the chaos of daily life, the mind often becomes a battleground of thoughts, worries, and stresses. Understanding the significance of cultivating a calm mind involves recognizing the profound impact it has on overall health and happiness. A calm mind serves as a sanctuary amidst the storm, allowing individuals to navigate challenges with greater clarity and resilience.

Enhanced Mental Clarity: A calm mind facilitates clearer thinking and decision-making. When the mind is free from the noise of stress, individuals can approach problems with a more focused and rational perspective.

Stress Reduction: Chronic stress is a prevalent issue in today's society, contributing to various health problems. Calming the mind is a powerful antidote to stress, as it helps regulate the body's stress response, reducing the risk of stress-related illnesses.

Improved Emotional Well-being: A calm mind fosters emotional stability, enabling individuals to manage their emotions more effectively. This, in turn, promotes healthier relationships and a more positive outlook on life.

Enhanced Creativity: The stillness of a calm mind provides a fertile ground for creativity to flourish. Ideas flow more freely when the mind is not clouded by stress or anxiety.

Benefits of Calming the Mind

Calming the mind is not just a temporary escape; it's a transformative practice that yields a myriad of benefits across various aspects of life. The advantages extend beyond momentary relief, influencing long-term well-being and personal growth.

Physical Health: Numerous studies link a calm mind to improved physical health. Reduced stress levels contribute to better cardiovascular health, immune function, and overall longevity.

Enhanced Sleep Quality: Calming practices promote relaxation, making it easier to achieve restful sleep. Quality sleep, in turn, supports cognitive function, mood regulation, and overall vitality.

Increased Resilience: A calm mind fosters resilience in the face of life's challenges. Rather than succumbing to stressors, individuals with a calm mindset can adapt more effectively and bounce back from adversity.

Heightened Self-Awareness: Calming the mind often involves introspection and mindfulness. This heightened self-awareness allows individuals to understand their thoughts and emotions better, paving the way for personal growth and self-improvement.

Improved Focus and Productivity: A calm mind is better equipped to concentrate on tasks at hand. Whether at work or in personal pursuits, improved focus and productivity are natural by-products of a calm and centered mental state.

As we delve into the following sections, we will explore practical techniques and strategies to help individuals embark on the journey of calming the mind, unlocking its full potential for a healthier, more fulfilling life.

Note: *This article contains an affiliate link which means that if you purchase the product from this link, I will get a small commission without extra charge to you.*

https://a628epogqly7rdxhphvnabs7a6.hop.clickbank.net

Chapter 2: The Science of Calming

Understanding the intricate interplay between the mind and the body is crucial in unraveling the science behind calming practices. Delving into the neurobiology of stress and relaxation, exploring the impact of stress on both the mind and body, and deciphering how specific calming techniques influence brain chemistry offers valuable insights into the transformative power of these practices.

Neurobiology of Stress and Relaxation

The brain is a complex organ with intricate neural networks that govern various physiological and psychological responses. When faced with stressors, the brain's amygdala, a region associated with the processing of emotions, triggers the release of stress hormones, including cortisol and adrenaline. This activation sets off the body's "fight or flight" response, preparing it to confront or evade perceived threats.

The Amygdala's Role: Understanding how the amygdala responds to stress provides insight into the emotional and physiological aspects of the stress response. Calming practices aim to modulate the amygdala's activity, promoting a more balanced emotional state.

Prefrontal Cortex Engagement: The prefrontal cortex, responsible for executive functions such as decision-making and emotional regulation, plays a crucial role in calming the stress response. Calming techniques often engage and strengthen the prefrontal cortex, promoting emotional resilience.

Impact of Stress on the Mind and Body

Stress, when chronic and unmanaged, can have profound effects on both mental and physical health. Understanding these effects underscores the importance of implementing calming practices as a preventive and therapeutic measure.

Cognitive Impairment: Prolonged exposure to stress can impair cognitive function, leading to difficulties in concentration, memory, and decision-making. Calming practices aim to reverse or mitigate these cognitive effects by promoting relaxation and mental clarity.

Psychological Well-being: Chronic stress is linked to an increased risk of anxiety and depression. Calming the mind through mindfulness and relaxation techniques provides a holistic approach to improving psychological well-being.

Physical Health Consequences: Stress takes a toll on the body, contributing to conditions such as cardiovascular disease, digestive issues, and weakened immune function. Calming practices not only alleviate the immediate symptoms of stress but also contribute to long-term physical health.

How Calming Techniques Affect Brain Chemistry

The brain's chemistry is dynamic and responsive to external stimuli, including the intentional practices of calming the mind. Various techniques influence neurotransmitters, hormones, and neural pathways, creating a neurochemical environment conducive to relaxation and well-being.

Neurotransmitter Regulation: Calming practices, such as meditation and deep breathing, have been shown to regulate neurotransmitters like serotonin and GABA, which play key roles in mood regulation and relaxation.

Hormonal Balance: Cortisol, often elevated during periods of stress, is regulated through calming practices. Consistent engagement in relaxation techniques helps restore a healthy balance of cortisol, reducing the negative impacts of chronic stress.

Neuroplasticity: Calming practices promote neuroplasticity, the brain's ability to reorganize itself by forming new neural connections. This adaptability is harnessed to create positive changes in thought patterns and emotional responses.

In the subsequent sections, we will explore specific calming techniques that leverage these scientific principles to foster relaxation, resilience, and an overall sense of well-being. By understanding the science behind calming practices, individuals can approach these techniques with a deeper appreciation for their transformative potential on both the brain and the body.

Note: This article contains affiliate links which means that if you purchase the products from these links

Chapter 3:   Mindful Breathing Techniques

The art of mindful breathing serves as a cornerstone in the practice of calming the mind. These techniques harness the power of conscious breath to anchor attention in the present moment, promoting relaxation and a sense of inner calm. Here, we explore four powerful mindful breathing techniques: Deep Belly Breathing, Box Breathing, the 4-7-8 Technique, and Diaphragmatic Breathing.

Deep Belly Breathing

Deep Belly Breathing, also known as diaphragmatic breathing, involves intentionally directing the breath into the diaphragm rather than shallow chest breathing. This technique activates the body's relaxation response and is a fundamental practice in mindfulness.

Technique:

- Find a comfortable seated or lying position.
- Place one hand on your chest and the other on your abdomen.
- Inhale deeply through your nose, allowing your abdomen to expand.
- Exhale slowly through pursed lips, feeling your abdomen contract.
- Focus on the rhythmic rise and fall of your abdomen with each breath.

Benefits:

- Engages the diaphragm for efficient breathing.
- Increases oxygen intake, promoting relaxation.
- Alleviates tension in the chest and shoulders.

Box Breathing

Box Breathing, also known as square breathing, is a structured technique that helps regulate the breath, calm the nervous system, and enhance focus. It involves equal durations for inhalation, holding the breath, exhalation, and holding the breath again.

Technique:

- Inhale through the nose for a count of four.
- Hold the breath for a count of four.
- Exhale through the mouth or nose for a count of four.
- Hold the breath for a count of four before beginning the next cycle.

Benefits:

- Promotes a balanced and steady breath.
- Enhances concentration and mindfulness.
- Alters the body's stress response.

4-7-8 Technique

Developed by Dr. Andrew Weil, the 4-7-8 Technique is a simple yet effective breathing exercise that combines specific counts for inhalation, holding the breath, and exhalation. It's designed to induce a sense of calm and relaxation.

Technique:

- Inhale quietly through your nose for a count of four.
- Hold your breath for a count of seven.
- Exhale completely through your mouth for a count of eight.
- Repeat the cycle at least three times.

Benefits:

- Promotes a sense of tranquility and balance.
- Slows down the heart rate.
- Facilitates a shift from the "fight or flight" response to the "rest and digest" state.

Diaphragmatic Breathing

Diaphragmatic Breathing, also known as abdominal or belly breathing, focuses on engaging the diaphragm to promote deep, relaxed breaths. This technique is particularly effective in reducing stress and increasing overall well-being.

Technique:

- Sit or lie down comfortably.
- Place one hand on your chest and the other on your abdomen.
- Inhale deeply through your nose, allowing your abdomen to rise.

- Exhale slowly through pursed lips, feeling your abdomen fall.
- Repeat for several breath cycles, maintaining a slow and steady rhythm.

Benefits:

- Enhances oxygenation of the body.
- Activates the body's relaxation response.
- Releases tension in the shoulders and neck.

Incorporating these mindful breathing techniques into your daily routine provides a practical and accessible way to cultivate a calm mind, reduce stress, and promote overall well-being. Experiment with each technique to discover which resonates most with you, and consider integrating them into moments of your day when you seek serenity and focus.

Chapter 4:   Meditation Practices

Meditation, with its roots in ancient contemplative traditions, has evolved into a diverse array of practices that contribute to the cultivation of a calm and centered mind. In this section, we explore four meditation techniques—Mindfulness Meditation, Loving-Kindness Meditation, Guided Imagery Meditation, and Body Scan Meditation—each offering unique approaches to inner peace, self-discovery, and emotional well-being.

Mindfulness Meditation

Mindfulness Meditation, rooted in Buddhist traditions, involves cultivating a non-judgmental awareness of the present moment. This practice encourages individuals to observe their thoughts and feelings without attachment, fostering a deep sense of presence.

Technique:

- Find a quiet space and sit comfortably.
- Focus your attention on your breath, sensations, or a chosen point of focus.
- When thoughts arise, gently redirect your attention without judgment.
- Practice sustained attention, gradually expanding your awareness to include your surroundings.

Benefits:

- Enhances present-moment awareness.
- Reduces stress and anxiety.
- Improves emotional regulation and cognitive function.

Loving-Kindness Meditation

Loving-Kindness Meditation, or Metta Meditation, stems from the Buddhist tradition and emphasizes the cultivation of compassion and love towards oneself and others. This practice involves directing positive intentions and well-wishes towards individuals and, ultimately, all beings.

Technique:

- Find a comfortable posture and close your eyes.
- Begin by focusing on feelings of love and kindness towards yourself.
- Extend these feelings to loved ones, acquaintances, and even those with whom you may have challenges.
- Broaden your scope to include all living beings, expressing goodwill and kindness.

Benefits:

- Cultivates feelings of compassion and empathy.
- Enhances positive emotions and reduces negative ones.
- Strengthens social connections and fosters a sense of interconnectedness.

Guided Imagery Meditation

Guided Imagery Meditation involves creating a mental landscape through vivid sensory imagery, often guided by a teacher, recording, or one's imagination. This practice utilizes the power of visualization to induce relaxation and stimulate the mind's creative capacities.

Technique:

- Find a quiet and comfortable space.
- Close your eyes and listen to a guided imagery meditation script or create your own.
- Imagine a serene and calming environment, engaging all your senses.
- Explore this mental landscape, allowing stress to dissipate and tranquility to emerge.

Benefits:

- Relaxes the mind and reduces stress.
- Enhances creative thinking and problem-solving skills.
- Provides a mental escape and fosters a sense of calm.

Body Scan Meditation

Body Scan Meditation is a mindfulness practice that involves systematically directing attention to different parts of the body, promoting awareness and relaxation. This technique is particularly effective in releasing physical tension and promoting a sense of embodiment.

Technique:

- Lie down in a comfortable position.
- Start with your toes and gradually move your attention up through each part of the body.
- Notice sensations without judgment, allowing tension to release.
- Continue scanning until you reach the top of your head.

Benefits:

- Promotes a heightened awareness of the body.
- Relieves physical tension and discomfort.
- Enhances the mind-body connection.

Incorporating these meditation practices into your routine allows you to explore various avenues of self-discovery and mental well-being. Whether you seek mindfulness, compassion, relaxation, or heightened awareness, these practices provide versatile tools for cultivating a calm and resilient mind. Experiment with each technique, and adapt them to suit your unique preferences and needs on your journey to inner peace.

Note: *This article contains an affiliate link which means that if you purchase the product from this link, I will get a small commission without extra charge to you.*

https://2cbeakffpa2wx-omva7gpk1ufy.hop.clickbank.net

Chapter 5:   Yoga for Tranquility

Yoga, with its holistic approach to physical and mental well-being, is a powerful practice for cultivating tranquility. This section explores three aspects of yoga that contribute to a calm mind—Gentle Yoga Poses, Flowing Sequences for Stress Reduction, and Yoga Nidra for Deep Relaxation—each offering a unique pathway to inner peace and serenity.

Gentle Yoga Poses

Gentle Yoga Poses provide a serene entry point into the practice, offering a combination of stretching, breathing, and mindfulness. These poses are accessible to individuals of all fitness levels and can be tailored to meet specific needs, making them an ideal starting point for those seeking tranquility through yoga.

Examples of Gentle Yoga Poses:

- Child's Pose (Balasana): A restful pose that stretches the back and promotes relaxation.
- Mountain Pose (Tadasana): A grounding pose that enhances posture and focus.
- Easy Pose (Sukhasana): A comfortable seated position for meditation and gentle stretching.

Benefits:

- Increases flexibility and range of motion.
- Relieves tension in the muscles.
- Encourages mindful breathing and relaxation.

Flowing Sequences for Stress Reduction

Flowing Sequences involve a series of poses linked together in a fluid and intentional manner, synchronized with breath. These sequences are designed to create a moving meditation, promoting a sense of harmony between the body and mind. Flowing yoga practices are particularly effective for stress reduction and promoting mental clarity.

Example Flowing Sequence:

- Sun Salutation (Surya Namaskar): A dynamic sequence that warms up the body and connects breath with movement.
- Warrior Flow: Incorporating Warrior I, Warrior II, and Warrior III poses to build strength and focus.
- Seated Forward Bend (Paschimottanasana) to Child's Pose: A grounding sequence to release tension in the spine and promote relaxation.

Benefits:

- Enhances circulation and energy flow.
- Reduces stress and promotes a calm state of mind.
- Builds strength, flexibility, and resilience.

Yoga Nidra for Deep Relaxation

Yoga Nidra, often referred to as "yogic sleep," is a guided meditation practice that induces a state of deep relaxation and inner calm. This technique involves systematic body scanning, breath awareness, and visualization to facilitate a profound release of tension and stress.

Yoga Nidra Process:

- Set an Intention: Establish a positive intention or Sankalpa for the practice.
- Body Scan: Bring awareness to different parts of the body, releasing tension.
- Breath Awareness: Focus on the natural flow of breath, promoting relaxation.
- Visualization: Engage the mind in guided imagery to enhance tranquility.
- Deep Relaxation: Enter a state of profound rest, akin to a deep and rejuvenating sleep.

Benefits:

- Reduces stress, anxiety, and insomnia.
- Enhances emotional well-being and clarity of mind.
- Promotes a sense of inner peace and rejuvenation.

Incorporating these elements of yoga into your routine provides a holistic approach to cultivating tranquility. Whether through gentle poses, flowing sequences, or the profound relaxation of Yoga Nidra, yoga offers a versatile toolkit for fostering a calm and centered mind. Explore these practices with an open heart and a receptive mind, allowing the transformative power of yoga to unfold in your journey toward inner peace.

Chapter 6:   The Power of Visualization

Visualization is a potent tool that harnesses the mind's capacity to create mental images, fostering a profound connection between thought and emotion. This section explores three aspects of the power of visualization—Creating Mental Sanctuaries, Positive Affirmations, and Visualization Techniques for Stress Reduction—each offering a unique avenue for cultivating a calm and resilient mind.

Creating Mental Sanctuaries

Creating Mental Sanctuaries involves constructing vivid and peaceful mental images that serve as retreats for the mind. These sanctuaries provide a refuge from the stresses of daily life, offering a virtual space for relaxation and rejuvenation.

Steps to Create a Mental Sanctuary:

- Choose a Setting: Select a location that resonates with tranquility, such as a beach, forest, or mountaintop.
- Engage the Senses: Populate your sanctuary with sensory details—sounds of waves, rustling leaves, or the scent of flowers.
- Personalize the Space: Add elements that bring joy and calmness, like a comfortable chair, soothing colors, or cherished objects.

- Visit Regularly: Close your eyes and mentally transport yourself to your sanctuary, immersing yourself in its peaceful ambiance.

Benefits:

- Reduces stress and anxiety.
- Enhances the ability to manage challenging situations.
- Provides a quick and accessible mental escape.

Positive Affirmations

Positive Affirmations involve the conscious repetition of positive statements to cultivate a positive mindset and self-belief. These affirmations can counter negative thought patterns and contribute to a more optimistic and resilient outlook on life.

Examples of Positive Affirmations:

- "I am calm, centered, and in control of my thoughts and emotions."
- "I embrace challenges as opportunities for growth and learning."
- "My mind is clear, and I approach each day with a positive attitude."

Best Practices:

- Make Them Personal: Tailor affirmations to address specific areas of concern or self-improvement.

- Repeat Regularly: Integrate affirmations into daily routines, repeating them with conviction and intention.
- Believe in Their Power: Embrace affirmations as a means to shape your mindset and influence your emotional state.

Benefits:

- Builds self-confidence and self-esteem.
- Counteracts negative thought patterns.
- Encourages a positive and optimistic mindset.

Visualization Techniques for Stress Reduction

Visualization Techniques for Stress Reduction involve using mental imagery to alleviate stress and promote a sense of calm. These techniques range from visualizing the release of tension to envisioning a desired outcome, empowering individuals to actively influence their emotional and physical well-being.

Breathing Visualization:

- Inhale deeply, imagining clean and calming energy entering your body.
- Exhale slowly, visualizing stress and tension leaving with each breath.

Outcome Visualization:

- Envision a positive outcome in a challenging situation.
- Picture yourself handling the situation with calmness and competence.

Nature Visualization:

- Picture a serene natural setting, like a peaceful forest or a tranquil lake.
- Engage your senses by imagining the sights, sounds, and smells of this calming environment.

Benefits:

- Reduces physiological markers of stress, such as heart rate and cortisol levels.
- Enhances relaxation and mental clarity.
- Empowers individuals to manage stress actively.

Incorporating visualization into your daily routine provides a powerful means to influence your thoughts, emotions, and overall well-being. Whether creating mental sanctuaries, using positive affirmations, or employing visualization techniques for stress reduction, the mind's ability to create and embrace positive mental imagery contributes significantly to the cultivation of a calm and resilient mindset.

Chapter 7:   Mindfulness in Daily Life

The essence of mindfulness extends beyond formal meditation sessions, encompassing a way of being that infuses everyday activities with awareness and presence. In this section, we explore three aspects of integrating mindfulness into daily life—Bringing Mindfulness to Everyday Activities, Mindful Eating, and Mindful Walking—each offering practical ways to cultivate a mindful and centered existence.

Bringing Mindfulness to Everyday Activities

Mindfulness in daily life involves infusing routine tasks and moments with intentional awareness. By being fully present in each moment, individuals can transform ordinary activities into opportunities for calmness and clarity.

Practical Examples:

- Mindful Breathing: Take a few moments to focus on your breath while waiting in line, commuting, or during daily chores.
- Observing Surroundings: Notice the sights, sounds, and sensations in your environment without judgment as you move through your day.
- Single-Tasking: Rather than multitasking, commit to one task at a time, giving it your full attention.

Benefits:

- Enhances focus and concentration.
- Reduces stress by promoting a sense of presence.
- Cultivates gratitude for everyday experiences.

Mindful Eating

Mindful Eating is a practice that involves bringing full attention to the experience of eating, from the selection of food to the act of chewing and savoring each bite. This practice fosters a healthier relationship with food and a heightened awareness of the sensory aspects of eating.

Steps for Mindful Eating:

- Conscious Food Selection: Consider the colors, textures, and nutritional value of the food you choose.
- Savoring Each Bite: Chew slowly and pay attention to the flavors, textures, and sensations.
- Engaging the Senses: Use all your senses to fully experience the meal, appreciating the aroma, taste, and even the sounds of eating.
- Listening to Hunger Cues: Tune into your body's signals of hunger and fullness.

Benefits:

- Promotes healthier eating habits.
- Reduces overeating and supports weight management.

- Enhances appreciation for the sensory pleasures of food.

Mindful Walking

Mindful Walking is a practice that involves bringing attention to each step and the sensations associated with walking. Whether indoors or outdoors, this practice encourages individuals to be fully present in the act of walking, fostering a sense of groundedness and tranquility.

Mindful Walking Techniques:

- Conscious Steps: Walk at a slower pace, paying attention to the sensation of each step.
- Breath Awareness: Sync your breath with your steps, inhaling and exhaling in a relaxed rhythm.
- Observing Surroundings: Notice the sights, sounds, and smells around you as you walk.
- Walking Meditation: Turn your walk into a meditation by maintaining a focused awareness on each step.

Benefits:

- Enhances physical well-being by promoting movement and circulation.
- Reduces mental chatter and promotes a sense of calm.
- Cultivates a mindful approach to movement in everyday life.

Incorporating mindfulness into daily activities offers a pathway to infuse each moment with a sense of awareness and presence. Whether bringing mindfulness to routine tasks, practicing mindful eating, or embracing the art of mindful walking, these practices contribute to a more grounded and centered way of life. The key lies in approaching each activity with a beginner's mind and a commitment to being fully present in the richness of each moment.

Chapter 8:   Digital Detox and Mindfulness

In the age of constant connectivity and digital engagement, incorporating a digital detox and mindful technology use into our lives has become increasingly essential. This section explores three aspects of maintaining a healthy relationship with technology—Reducing Screen Time, Mindful Technology Use, and Creating Digital-Free Spaces—each offering strategies to balance the benefits of technology with the need for mindfulness and presence.

Reducing Screen Time

Reducing Screen Time involves consciously limiting the amount of time spent on digital devices such as smartphones, computers, and tablets. This practice aims to mitigate the potential negative effects of excessive screen exposure, including eye strain, disrupted sleep patterns, and decreased face-to-face social interactions.

Strategies for Reducing Screen Time:

- Set Boundaries: Establish specific time limits for device use, especially during leisure hours.
- Unplug Before Bed: Create a screen-free period before bedtime to improve sleep quality.
- Implement Tech-Free Zones: Designate certain areas of your home, such as the bedroom or dining area, as tech-free zones.

Benefits:

- Improves overall well-being by reducing digital fatigue.
- Enhances quality of sleep and circadian rhythm.
- Encourages more meaningful face-to-face interactions.

Mindful Technology Use

Mindful Technology Use involves approaching digital interactions with intentionality and presence. Instead of mindlessly scrolling through screens, individuals can cultivate awareness and conscious engagement with technology, fostering a more positive and intentional relationship with their devices.

Practices for Mindful Technology Use:

- Set Intentions: Clarify your purpose before using technology, whether it's for work, communication, or leisure.
- Practice Digital Sabbaths: Dedicate specific time periods or days for complete digital disconnection.
- Mindful Notifications: Turn off non-essential notifications to minimize distractions and interruptions.

Benefits:

- Enhances focus and productivity by reducing multitasking.
- Promotes healthier relationships with technology.

- Cultivates a sense of control and intentionality in digital interactions.

Creating Digital-Free Spaces

Creating Digital-Free Spaces involves designating specific areas or times where technology is intentionally excluded. This practice allows individuals to carve out spaces for undistracted and mindful activities, fostering a deeper connection with the present moment.

Examples of Digital-Free Spaces:

- Mealtime: Designate mealtime as a tech-free zone to promote mindful eating and meaningful conversation.
- Bedroom: Keep digital devices out of the bedroom to create a serene and restful environment.
- Nature Retreats: When spending time in nature, make an intentional effort to disconnect from screens and embrace the natural surroundings.

Benefits:

- Supports mental well-being by providing breaks from constant digital stimulation.
- Fosters deeper connections in relationships by removing digital distractions.
- Encourages engagement with the present moment and the physical environment.

By incorporating these strategies into our daily lives, we can strike a balance between the advantages of technology and the need for mindful, intentional living. A conscious digital detox, coupled with mindful technology use and the creation of digital-free spaces, empowers individuals to reclaim control over their relationship with technology and foster a more mindful and balanced approach to the digital age.

Chapter 9:   Art and Creativity for Relaxation

Engaging in artistic and creative pursuits has proven to be a therapeutic and enjoyable way to promote relaxation, reduce stress, and enhance overall well-being. This section explores three avenues for using art and creativity as tools for relaxation—Coloring and Drawing, Journaling and Creative Writing, and Expressive Arts Therapy—each offering unique approaches to tapping into the healing power of self-expression.

Coloring and Drawing

Coloring and Drawing are simple yet effective ways to channel creativity and promote relaxation. These activities tap into the meditative qualities of focused creation, allowing individuals to express themselves visually without the pressure of creating a masterpiece.

Coloring and Drawing Techniques:

- Mindful Coloring: Choose a coloring book or printable pages and immerse yourself in the process, paying attention to each stroke and color choice.
- Freeform Drawing: Allow your imagination to guide your hand as you draw without specific expectations or goals.
- Mandala Creation: Design intricate mandalas or use pre-made templates to engage in a structured and calming creative practice.

Benefits:

- Relaxes the mind and fosters mindfulness.
- Provides an outlet for self-expression and creativity.
- Encourages a sense of accomplishment and satisfaction.

Journaling and Creative Writing

Journaling and Creative Writing offer an opportunity for introspection, self-discovery, and emotional expression. Whether through daily reflections, poetry, or storytelling, the act of putting thoughts into words can be a therapeutic and cathartic practice.

Journaling and Creative Writing Prompts:

- Gratitude Journaling: Write about things you are thankful for each day.
- Stream-of-Consciousness Writing: Let your thoughts flow freely onto the paper without worrying about structure or grammar.
- Storytelling: Create fictional worlds and characters through short stories or narrative prose.

Benefits:

- Provides an emotional outlet for processing feelings and experiences.
- Enhances self-awareness and introspection.
- Fosters creativity and imagination.

Expressive Arts Therapy

Expressive Arts Therapy involves engaging in various art forms, such as visual arts, music, dance, and drama, to explore and communicate emotions. This therapeutic approach encourages individuals to express themselves through artistic mediums as a means of self-discovery and healing.

Modalities of Expressive Arts Therapy:

- Visual Arts: Painting, drawing, and sculpture to express emotions visually.
- Music Therapy: Creating and listening to music as a way to process emotions.
- Movement Therapy: Using dance and movement to explore and release tension.
- Drama Therapy: Role-playing and storytelling to gain insight into personal narratives.

Benefits:

- Integrates the mind, body, and emotions in the therapeutic process.
- Provides a safe and non-verbal space for expression.
- Facilitates personal growth and healing.

Incorporating art and creativity into relaxation practices offers a dynamic and enjoyable way to manage stress and enhance well-being. Whether through coloring and drawing, journaling and creative writing, or engaging in expressive arts therapy, these activities tap into the transformative power of self-expression, providing a pathway to relaxation, self-discovery, and emotional release.

Note: This article contains an affiliate link which means that if you purchase the product from this link, I will get a small commission without extra charge to you.

https://c2abddh6skw-l0plk8yewidy5u.hop.clickbank.net

Chapter 10: Natural Remedies for a Calm Mind

In the quest for a calm mind, nature provides a wealth of remedies that harness the soothing power of plants. This section explores three natural approaches to promote tranquility—Herbal Teas and Infusions, Aromatherapy, and Adaptogenic Herbs for Stress Relief—each offering gentle and holistic methods to support a serene state of mind.

Herbal Teas and Infusions

Herbal Teas and Infusions have been cherished for centuries for their calming properties and therapeutic benefits. From soothing blends to single-ingredient infusions, these beverages offer a comforting and natural way to promote relaxation.

Common Calming Herbs for Tea:

- Chamomile: Known for its gentle sedative properties, chamomile tea aids in relaxation and sleep.
- Lavender: Lavender-infused tea is celebrated for its calming and stress-reducing effects.
- Peppermint: Besides aiding digestion, peppermint tea can have a calming influence on the mind.
- Valerian Root: Often used to address insomnia and promote relaxation.

Preparation Tips:

- Steeping Time: Follow recommended steeping times for optimal flavor and benefits.

- Mindful Sipping: Embrace the ritual of sipping tea slowly to enhance the calming experience.
- Experiment with Blends: Combine different herbs to create your personalized calming blend.

Benefits:

- Promotes relaxation and stress reduction.
- Supports better sleep and digestion.
- Provides a comforting and ritualistic experience.

Aromatherapy

Aromatherapy harnesses the aromatic compounds of essential oils to stimulate the olfactory system, influencing mood and emotions. Incorporating the scents of calming essential oils into your environment can be a powerful tool for creating a tranquil atmosphere.

Calming Essential Oils:

- Lavender: Renowned for its relaxing properties, lavender promotes calmness and reduces anxiety.
- Frankincense: This earthy scent is known to induce a sense of peace and spiritual grounding.
- Bergamot: Citrusy and uplifting, bergamot essential oil can help alleviate stress and elevate mood.
- Chamomile: The soothing aroma of chamomile contributes to relaxation and emotional balance.

Application Methods:

- Diffusion: Use an essential oil diffuser to disperse calming scents throughout a room.
- Topical Application: Dilute essential oils with a carrier oil and apply to pulse points or temples.
- Aromatic Baths: Add a few drops of calming essential oils to a warm bath for a relaxing soak.

Benefits:

- Elicits a calming response in the nervous system.
- Creates a serene and inviting atmosphere.
- Supports emotional well-being and stress relief.

Adaptogenic Herbs for Stress Relief

Adaptogenic Herbs are known for their ability to help the body adapt to stress and promote balance. These herbs, often used in traditional medicine systems like Ayurveda and Traditional Chinese Medicine, work holistically to support the body's resilience to stressors.

Common Adaptogenic Herbs:

- Rhodiola Rosea: Helps the body adapt to physical and emotional stress, promoting resilience.
- Ashwagandha: Traditionally used to reduce stress, anxiety, and promote overall well-being.
- Holy Basil (Tulsi): Revered in Ayurveda, tulsi supports the body's response to stress and balances energy.

- Eleuthero (Siberian Ginseng): Known for its adaptogenic properties, eleuthero enhances the body's ability to cope with stress.

Usage Recommendations:

- Supplements: Adaptogenic herbs are available in supplement form, following recommended dosages.
- Herbal Teas: Some adaptogens can be consumed as herbal teas or infusions.
- Consultation: It's advisable to consult with a healthcare professional before incorporating adaptogens, especially if you have pre-existing health conditions or take medications.

Benefits:

- Enhances the body's resilience to stressors.
- Promotes hormonal balance and supports the adrenal glands.
- Contributes to overall well-being and vitality.

Incorporating these natural remedies into your routine offers a holistic and gentle approach to calming the mind. Whether through the ritual of herbal teas, the ambiance of aromatherapy, or the adaptogenic support of herbs, nature provides a myriad of tools to help you find tranquility amidst the demands of daily life. As with any wellness practices, it's advisable to consult with a healthcare professional, particularly if you have specific health concerns or conditions.

Note: *This article contains an affiliate link which means that if you purchase the product from this link.*
https://0a9cfghash17s1u103ylo6bu63.hop.clickbank.net

Chapter 11: Creating a Tranquil Environment

The physical spaces we inhabit play a significant role in influencing our mental and emotional well-being. Crafting a tranquil environment involves intentional choices and design elements that promote relaxation and serenity. In this section, we explore three strategies for cultivating a calming atmosphere—Decluttering Spaces, Incorporating Relaxing Colors, and Using Soft Lighting.

Decluttering Spaces

A cluttered environment can contribute to feelings of overwhelm and stress. Decluttering is a powerful way to create a sense of order and tranquility, allowing for a clearer and more focused mind.

Steps for Decluttering:

- Set Clear Goals: Identify specific areas or items to declutter and set achievable goals.
- Organize Thoughtfully: Arrange items in an organized manner, utilizing storage solutions and containers.
- Minimize Distractions: Keep only the essentials in your immediate workspace to reduce visual noise.
- Regular Maintenance: Develop a routine for maintaining a clutter-free environment.

Benefits:

- Creates a sense of order and organization.
- Reduces visual stress and promotes mental clarity.

- Enhances the overall aesthetic of the space.

Incorporating Relaxing Colors

Color has a profound impact on mood and emotions. Incorporating calming and soothing colors into your environment can contribute significantly to the creation of a tranquil atmosphere.

Relaxing Colors:

- Soft Blues and Greens: Evoke a sense of calmness and connection with nature.
- Neutral Tones: Shades of beige, gray, and taupe create a serene and timeless backdrop.
- Muted Pastels: Gentle pastel hues like lavender and peach promote a soothing ambiance.
- Earth Tones: Browns, greens, and warm neutrals provide a grounding and comforting feel.

Application Tips:

- Feature Wall: Use a calming color as an accent on a focal wall.
- Soft Furnishings: Incorporate relaxing colors through cushions, throws, and curtains.
- Natural Elements: Bring in plants and natural materials to complement the color scheme.

Benefits:

- Influences mood and emotional well-being.
- Creates a visually harmonious and calming environment.

- Enhances the overall aesthetic appeal of the space.

Using Soft Lighting

Lighting is a key element in establishing the mood of a space. Soft, diffused lighting contributes to a cozy and tranquil atmosphere, reducing harsh contrasts and creating a more inviting environment.

Soft Lighting Options:

- Warm LED Bulbs: Opt for warm-toned bulbs to create a soft and comforting glow.
- Table Lamps and Floor Lamps: Place lamps strategically to create pockets of soft light.
- Candles and Diffusers: Use scented candles or essential oil diffusers for both light and aromatherapy.
- Indirect Lighting: Install fixtures that direct light upwards or towards walls to reduce glare.

Placement Strategies:

- Layered Lighting: Combine different sources of light for a balanced and layered effect.
- Dimmer Switches: Install dimmer switches for adjustable lighting levels.
- Task Lighting: Incorporate focused lighting for specific activities, like reading or working.

Benefits:

- Fosters a cozy and inviting atmosphere.
- Reduces eye strain and promotes relaxation.

- Enhances the ambiance of the space during different times of the day.

Incorporating these strategies into your living or working spaces can have a transformative effect on your daily experience. Whether through decluttering, choosing calming colors, or using soft lighting, intentional design choices contribute to the creation of an environment that supports relaxation and tranquility. Experiment with these elements to discover the combination that resonates most with your personal preferences and enhances your overall well-being.

Chapter 12: Mind-Body Connection

The mind and body are intricately connected, and nurturing this relationship is crucial for overall well-being. This section explores three facets of the mind-body connection—Importance of Physical Exercise, Holistic Health Practices, and Integrating Nutrition for Mental Well-being—each contributing to a harmonious and balanced relationship between the mental and physical aspects of health.

Importance of Physical Exercise

Physical exercise is a cornerstone of a healthy mind-body connection, offering a myriad of benefits for mental and physical well-being. Regular exercise has a profound impact on mood, cognition, and stress resilience.

Benefits of Physical Exercise:

- Mood Enhancement: Exercise stimulates the release of endorphins, neurotransmitters that promote feelings of happiness and well-being.
- Stress Reduction: Physical activity helps alleviate stress by reducing cortisol levels and promoting relaxation.
- Cognitive Function: Regular exercise has been linked to improved cognitive function, including memory and attention.
- Better Sleep: Engaging in physical activity contributes to better sleep quality, fostering overall mental health.

Types of Physical Exercise:

- Aerobic Exercise: Activities like running, swimming, or cycling that elevate the heart rate and improve cardiovascular health.
- Strength Training: Building muscle through resistance exercises to enhance overall physical health.
- Mindful Movement: Practices like yoga or tai chi that combine physical activity with mindfulness.

Incorporating Exercise into Daily Life:

- Set Realistic Goals: Establish achievable exercise goals to make physical activity a sustainable part of your routine.
- Variety: Explore different forms of exercise to keep it interesting and target various muscle groups.
- Mindful Movement: Incorporate mindful movement practices to combine physical activity with mental relaxation.

Holistic Health Practices

Holistic health practices emphasize the interconnectedness of the mind, body, and spirit. These practices, which often draw from traditional healing systems, aim to promote overall well-being by addressing multiple dimensions of health.

Holistic Health Practices:

- Meditation and Mindfulness: Cultivate present-moment awareness to promote mental clarity and emotional balance.
- Acupuncture: An ancient Chinese practice involving the insertion of thin needles into specific points on the body to balance energy flow.
- Chiropractic Care: Focuses on the relationship between the spine and the nervous system to optimize overall health.
- Biofeedback: Utilizes technology to provide real-time information about physiological processes, helping individuals gain control over bodily functions.

Benefits of Holistic Health Practices:

- Stress Reduction: Holistic practices often include techniques for stress management and relaxation.
- Enhanced Mind-Body Awareness: Practices like meditation foster a deeper connection between the mind and body.
- Promotion of Energy Flow: Modalities like acupuncture aim to balance the body's energy flow for optimal health.

Incorporating Holistic Practices:

- Explore Different Modalities: Experiment with various holistic practices to discover what resonates with you.

- Consistency: Integrate these practices into your routine consistently for long-term benefits.
- Mindful Engagement: Approach each practice with an open and mindful mindset, focusing on the present experience.

Integrating Nutrition for Mental Well-being

Nutrition plays a vital role in supporting mental well-being, influencing neurotransmitter production, brain function, and overall mood. A well-balanced and nourishing diet contributes to a healthy mind-body connection.

Nutritional Strategies for Mental Well-being:

- Balanced Diet: Consume a variety of nutrient-dense foods, including fruits, vegetables, whole grains, lean proteins, and healthy fats.
- Omega-3 Fatty Acids: Found in fatty fish, flaxseeds, and walnuts, omega-3s support brain health and may help alleviate symptoms of depression.
- Complex Carbohydrates: Opt for whole grains and complex carbohydrates, which provide a steady release of energy and support serotonin production.
- Hydration: Maintain adequate hydration, as even mild dehydration can impact mood and cognitive function.

Mindful Eating Practices:

- Savoring Each Bite: Eat slowly and mindfully, paying attention to the flavors, textures, and sensations of each bite.

- Balanced Portions: Practice portion control and listen to your body's hunger and fullness cues.
- Emotional Connection: Be mindful of emotional eating patterns and address the root causes of cravings.

Consultation with Nutrition Professionals:

- Registered Dietitian: Seek guidance from a registered dietitian for personalized nutrition advice.
- Nutritional Psychiatry: Explore the emerging field of nutritional psychiatry, which examines the impact of diet on mental health.

In conclusion, fostering a strong mind-body connection involves a holistic approach that encompasses physical activity, holistic health practices, and mindful nutrition. By recognizing the interconnectedness of these elements, individuals can cultivate a balanced and resilient foundation for overall well-being. Experiment with different practices and strategies to discover what aligns with your preferences and contributes to a harmonious mind-body connection.

Note: *This article contains an affiliate link which means that if you purchase the product from this link, I will get a small commission without extra charge to you.*

https://ae407qqcq8y8q5rlfm4jp1loay.hop.clickbank.net

Chapter 13: Building Resilience

Resilience is the ability to bounce back from adversity, adapt to challenges, and grow stronger in the face of setbacks. This section explores three key aspects of building resilience—Developing Emotional Resilience, Cultivating a Positive Mindset, and Learning from Challenges—each contributing to the development of a resilient and adaptable mindset.

Developing Emotional Resilience

Emotional resilience involves the ability to navigate and manage emotions effectively, even in the midst of challenging situations. By developing emotional resilience, individuals can maintain a sense of equilibrium and respond to stressors in a healthy and adaptive way.

Strategies for Developing Emotional Resilience:

- Self-awareness: Understand and identify your emotions without judgment.
- Emotional Regulation: Learn healthy coping mechanisms for managing stress and negative emotions.
- Cultivate Empathy: Understand others' perspectives and build meaningful connections.
- Mindfulness Practices: Engage in mindfulness and meditation to stay present and centered.

Benefits of Emotional Resilience:

- Better Stress Management: Respond to stressors with composure and adaptability.
- Improved Relationships: Foster stronger connections with others through empathetic understanding.
- Enhanced Emotional Well-being: Develop a more positive and balanced emotional state.

Cultivating a Positive Mindset

A positive mindset involves approaching challenges with optimism, viewing setbacks as opportunities for growth, and maintaining a hopeful outlook. Cultivating a positive mindset contributes significantly to building resilience.

Practices for Cultivating a Positive Mindset:

- Gratitude Journaling: Reflect on and appreciate the positive aspects of your life.
- Optimistic Thinking: Challenge negative thoughts and reframe them in a more positive light.
- Visualization: Envision successful outcomes and focus on the possibilities for positive change.
- Affirmations: Use positive affirmations to reinforce optimistic beliefs about yourself and your capabilities.

Benefits of a Positive Mindset:

- Increased Resilience: Approach challenges with a mindset geared towards growth and learning.
- Enhanced Mental Well-being: Reduce the impact of stress by maintaining a positive outlook.
- Improved Problem-Solving: Find creative solutions by approaching difficulties with optimism.

Learning from Challenges

Resilience involves not just bouncing back from adversity but also learning and growing from the experience. Embracing challenges as opportunities for learning and personal development is a key aspect of building resilience.

Approaches for Learning from Challenges:

- Reflective Practices: Take time to reflect on challenges, identifying lessons learned and areas for growth.
- Adaptive Problem-Solving: Approach challenges with a solution-oriented mindset, focusing on what can be changed.
- Seeking Support: Reach out to others for guidance and perspective during challenging times.
- Maintaining Perspective: View setbacks as temporary and consider the bigger picture.

Benefits of Learning from Challenges:

- Continuous Growth: Develop a mindset that values continuous learning and improvement.
- Increased Adaptability: Become more flexible and adaptable in the face of change.

- Resilient Problem-Solving: Apply insights gained from challenges to navigate future difficulties more effectively.

Incorporating these strategies into daily life can contribute to the development of a resilient mindset. By focusing on emotional resilience, cultivating a positive mindset, and approaching challenges as opportunities for growth, individuals can build the capacity to navigate life's ups and downs with greater adaptability and strength. Remember that resilience is a skill that can be developed over time through intentional effort and practice.

Chapter 14: Connecting with Others

Human connection is a fundamental aspect of well-being, impacting mental, emotional, and even physical health. This section explores three elements of connecting with others—Importance of Social Support, Communicating Mindfully, and Building Healthy Relationships—each contributing to the creation of meaningful and supportive connections.

Importance of Social Support

Social support refers to the network of relationships that provide emotional, instrumental, and informational assistance. Cultivating a strong social support system is vital for mental and emotional well-being, offering a safety net during challenging times.

Benefits of Social Support:

- Emotional Resilience: Having a support system fosters emotional strength and the ability to cope with stress.
- Reduced Feelings of Isolation: Connection with others helps combat loneliness and feelings of isolation.
- Improved Mental Health: Strong social ties are linked to lower rates of anxiety and depression.
- Enhanced Physical Health: Social support contributes to better overall health and longevity.

Ways to Cultivate Social Support:

- Maintain Relationships: Nurture existing connections with friends, family, and colleagues.
- Join Communities: Engage in activities or groups aligned with your interests to meet like-minded individuals.
- Express Vulnerability: Be open and honest about your feelings, allowing others to provide support.
- Offer Support: Building strong connections involves reciprocity—offer support to others in times of need.

Communicating Mindfully

Effective communication is the foundation of healthy relationships. Mindful communication involves being present, listening actively, and expressing oneself with clarity and empathy.

Principles of Mindful Communication:

- Presence: Be fully present in conversations, giving your undivided attention.
- Active Listening: Focus on understanding the speaker's perspective before formulating your response.
- Non-Verbal Cues: Pay attention to body language and tone to grasp the full context of communication.
- Empathy: Seek to understand and validate others' emotions and experiences.
- Clarity: Express thoughts and feelings clearly and respectfully.

Benefits of Mindful Communication:

- Improved Connection: Mindful communication fosters deeper connections with others.
- Conflict Resolution: Effective communication is key to resolving conflicts and misunderstandings.
- Strengthened Relationships: Mindful communication contributes to the health and strength of relationships.

Building Healthy Relationships

Healthy relationships are built on mutual respect, trust, and open communication. Whether in friendships, family connections, or romantic partnerships, cultivating healthy relationships contributes to a supportive and fulfilling life.

Characteristics of Healthy Relationships:

- Respect: Treat others with consideration and value their perspectives.
- Trust: Build and maintain trust through honesty and reliability.
- Boundaries: Establish and respect personal boundaries for a healthy balance.
- Communication: Foster open and honest communication to strengthen the connection.
- Empathy: Understand and empathize with others' feelings and experiences.

Cultivating Healthy Relationships:

- Effective Communication: Address concerns openly and work together to find solutions.
- Quality Time: Spend quality time together, engaging in activities that strengthen the connection.
- Express Gratitude: Show appreciation for the positive aspects of the relationship.
- Mutual Growth: Encourage each other's personal and collective growth.

Benefits of Healthy Relationships:

- Emotional Support: Healthy relationships provide a source of emotional support during both good and challenging times.
- Increased Well-being: Positive connections contribute to overall life satisfaction and happiness.
- Resilience: Supportive relationships enhance the ability to navigate life's ups and downs.

In conclusion, the quality of our connections with others significantly influences our well-being. By recognizing the importance of social support, practicing mindful communication, and actively building healthy relationships, individuals can create a foundation of meaningful connections that contribute to a more fulfilling and resilient life.

Chapter 15: Conclusion

In the journey towards a calmer mind, resilient mindset, and meaningful connections, several key strategies have been explored. These practices are not just isolated activities but interconnected elements that contribute to holistic well-being. Let's offer encouragement for ongoing practice.

Encouragement for Ongoing Practice

Embarking on a journey to cultivate a calm mind, resilient mindset, and meaningful connections is a continuous process. It's essential to approach these practices with patience, self-compassion, and a commitment to personal growth. Here are some encouraging reminders:

Consistency Matters: The benefits of these practices often emerge with consistent effort. Incorporate them into your routine gradually and celebrate small victories along the way.

Adapt to Your Needs: Each individual is unique, and what works for one person may not work for another. Be open to exploring different strategies and adapting them to fit your preferences and lifestyle.

Mindfulness in Progress: Mindfulness is not about achieving perfection but cultivating awareness in the present moment. If your mind wanders or if a practice feels challenging, it's all part of the learning process.

Celebrate Progress: Recognize and celebrate the progress you make on your journey. Whether it's improved focus during meditation or building stronger connections with others, acknowledge the positive changes.

Seek Support: Don't hesitate to seek support from friends, family, or professionals. Share your experiences and learn from the wisdom of others on a similar path.

Embrace the Journey: The journey to a calmer mind, resilient mindset, and meaningful connections is ongoing. Embrace the journey, savor the moments of growth, and approach challenges as opportunities for learning and transformation.

Remember, these practices are not meant to be a quick fix but rather tools for ongoing self-discovery and well-being. As you continue to explore and integrate these strategies into your life, may you find a deeper sense of calm, resilience, and connection. The journey is uniquely yours, and each step forward is a testament to your commitment to a healthier and more fulfilling life.

Note: *This article contains affiliate links which means that if you purchase the product from these links, I will get a small commission without extra charge to you.*

https://c4727ko5max-ud2ovcp7xenjce.hop.clickbank.net